Breathe;

Gentle Whispers of Healing

I Wasn't Raised by People

The Mind Of A Child

A White Dove

The Power Of Words

I Know It's Not Easy

Our Lives...

who am i?

The Little Girl In Me

Failure

A Message To My Best Friend

My Reason

Freedom

painted.

Songs of Shattered Souls

100 Different Me's

In Another Reality

My Mother's Clone

just.take.the.pill.

It's All An Act

South African Inspired

Mzansi

Verhonger

Die Duiwel

Acknowledgements

About the Author

To little me... we did it.

I Wasn't Raised by People

I wasn't raised by people
Or at least I don't think
For if I was
I'd be angry and spiteful
Like those who influenced me
Rather I believe that stories paved the way
For me to become the woman I am today
Characters on paper
Villains and heroes
Taught me morals and values
To be honest and loyal
To be true and joyful
To scream and to cry
But to get up and still fly
I wasn't raised by people
Or at least I don't think
I was raised by my books
That taught me to be me

The Mind Of A Child

Oh, how I wish to have the mind of a child.
To be jolly and gleeful again
To see the world through those virtuous eyes
And at the little things just smile.
For with a child's mind maybe then
I'd be a little more free
Instead of always uneasy.
Oh, the mind of a child
Is a very unappreciated gift
Filled with imagination and ideas-
With a child's mind,
I wish to live.

A White Dove

A white dove-
A representative peace and love.
A white dove-
A beautiful miracle from above.
A white dove-
An error of what Gaia has done.
So why is it
That a creature so diverse
Is seen as a blessing and not a curse?
If that is the case with an albino
Columbiformes,
Then why do we shame the diverse before us?
Why do we fear dissimilarity
When such a diverse creature is a symbol for
tranquility?
If we can commend a dove simply for its
pigmentation,
We can surely respect our variation.
Differentiation is not something to be feared
Or to be seen as weird
But to be valued and cherished
As we can see thanks to our feathered friend.
A white dove-
A symbol for hope and femininity.
A white dove-
An inspiration
For our future generation.
A white dove-
That is me.

The Power Of Words

Although your words don't leave a physical
mark,
They leave permanent scars all over my heart.
Although it is true, from your words,
My skin will not bruise,
My confidence and happiness, I will lose
Although to you it may not seem, that your
words hurt as Much As a physical injury,
With every word that is said, an insecurity is
born in my head
Words have a lot of power
And used in the wrong hands could be a self-
belief that is Devoured.
Used correctly however,
Could be a whisper of self-belief that has been
turned on even Louder!
If there is someone who is hurting you
And you cannot get rid of them whatever you
do!
Just remember to never stoop down to their
level
And that;
One who has hurt the most others
Is one which that has felt the most negative of
this power.

I Know It's Not Easy

"That math test wasn't easy" you say,
Although I already know.
"To get up this morning wasn't easy" you say,
Although I already know.
"Life hasn't been easy" you say,
Although I already know.
All of these things, I do not know because
you've told me,
But because I have those struggles as my own.
I know that it's not easy
And that things are rough-
But I also know that you are a warrior
And will not give up when things are tough.
Life may have won a few battles,
But you will win the war.
Life may have gotten the upper hand this time
But you have the ultimate control.
If you believe, you will succeed
I know it and so should you.

Our Lives...

As the river is wide
And the mountains are high
As the dolphins dive
And eagles fly
Every critter and plant
Play a crucial part
In creating the world
That you and I both love
But even with every bit
Of nature in the palm of our hand
We are nothing without our wits
That are gained from
Stories
Experiences
Our Lives
So as our hair starts to grey
And our skin starts to crease
It is important to remember
That each mark
Wrinkle
And Scar
Are the words written
Carefully by a poet
To tell of our stories
Our Experiences
Our Lives...

who am i?

who am i
if not smart?
if the red ink on my paper
doesn't form an 'A'?
If teachers and peers
aren't blown away?
A personality formed
around results-
So, I ask again,
Who am I
if not smart?

The Little Girl In Me

She starts to cry
when someone yells at me.
She flinches in fear
at the loud noises I hear.
She seeks validation
from the authority around me.
She curses me with sensitivity -
to take everything to heart,
to care too much
and try too hard.
The little girl in me...
She squeals and giggles
when I am gifted flowers
She longs to swim
in the sea I jog beside
She beams with pride
whenever I make someone smile
She blesses me with sensitivity
a chance to smile and laugh
at things no matter how small
to be human
flaws and all

Failure

Why do I feel braver
in my dreams
and on paper?
I suppose I can (hide)
behind my pen
and in my mind.
No risk,
all reward
but in life-
i'm not so sure...
Although I do fear
failure so-
it's not enough
for Me to let my dreams
go...

A Message To My Best Friend

I guess I never said
thank you
for everything you have done
from mid-day laughs
to
midnight talks
from holding me
to
scolding me
from giggling about crushes
to
yelling "All boys are stupid!"
You hold a place
in the heart
you did not
b r e a k.
So, I say, again,
Thank you
my friend.

My Reason

I simply picked up a pen...
She taught me to express
my wants and needs in words,
to appreciate the beauty
of stories and of poems.

The inadmissible craving
to share my thoughts-
it runs in my blood,
resulting that with passion and drive
my veins flood.

My mother-
My mentor-
The reason,
I'm a writer.

Freedom

What does freedom look like?
A license?
Money?
No...
Rather a little white pill -
crushedandcompresed
chemicals and hormones -
a slightly bitter taste.
A little white pill
by the name-
Lamotrigine.
That's what freedom
looks like to
me.

painted.

Her eyes carry hurt
yet-
glisten with hope.
Her body is the canvas
on which her story is
painted-
scars and marks,
freckles and spots,
from head to toe,
and from skin to bone.
She is so much more
than carbon combinations-
she is the artistic piece
with which her
experiences are
painted.

Songs of Shattered Souls

They sing with
all their might-
a desperate plea
to save them right.
Instead-
the world
turns a blind eye
saying;
"What a weakness
it is to cry".
When in reality
we weep
ourselves to sleep
in the hopes that
when we awake
to be a little more at peace.

That Wasn't Love...

You said you
loved me...
But how could
that be true?
Love is kind
and protective.
Love is raw
and pure.
You treated me
with spite
and hurt
with false words
and deceit.
You did not, in fact, love me-
not in the way
I did you.

100 Different Me's

my me.
His me.
Her me.
To some,
i am a villain.
To some,
i am a hero.
To my parents,
i am a daughter.
To my siblings,
i am a sister.
To an admirer,
i am a crush.
To a crush,
i am an admirer.
Out of the 100
different me's-
you're the only one
who really sees
the raw,
the true,
the authentic,
Me.

In Another Reality

In another reality,
there would be no me.
I would have died,
at 9
or at 11,
my life, no longer Mine.
There would be no you and me,
there would be no book.
It would have left my parents
permanently shook.
But we are not
in another reality.
We are in this one
(thankfully)-
where there is a you and Me,
where there is a book,
and my parents
are not shook.

A Better Revenge

I always thought
revenge to be,
loud and angry
cruel and mean.
"An eye for an eye"
or something like that
but-
now I know
revenge to be,
succeeding and thriving
when on my pain
they used to prey.

The Savior I Needed.

You become the woman,
you needed as a girl.
So, I suppose that's
the reason why I-
listen intently to people,
stand up for the underdog,
tell everyone that they are
more than enough,
and why I take on
other's burdens.
Because that is the woman
I needed to come and
save
me.

Your Life, Once Mine.

I see her in you-
the little girl I once was.
In your curious eyes
and your bunny smile.
In your struggles
no one else understands.
In your desperate prayers
for God to remove your
odd ways.
I see her in you-
the little girl I once was-
with all but one difference,
you have a mentor and support system-
I,
did not.

My Mother's Clone

I am my father's daughter.
I carry his eyes and name.
I speak his language
and use his slang.
But I am my mother's clone;
the way we write,
the way we walk,
the shared passion for justice,
the empathy we feel...
I am my father's daughter.
But I am my mother's clone...

just.take.the.pill.

I am a s h e l l-
a delicate casing
of a hollow being
I cannot identify-
of someone hidden
deep
down
inside,
trappedandconfined
in the back of my mind-
guarded by hormones and chemicals
plastered with
"helpful" claims.

It's All An Act

Smile, nod
and laugh politely
at jokes you don't
believe are funny.
"Good and you?"
is your new tagline,
if anyone asks you;
"How is life?"
It's common courtesy-
a part of humanity and
social etiquette
But-
why should I let
unspoken laws
sugar coat my raw
personality
all in the name of a "formality"?
When everybody knows
that it's all just for show.
I will not water myself
down
to look pretty on your shelf
on my individuality-
you.
Can.
Choke.

South African Inspired

Mzansi

Springboks prance.
The Blue cranes

soar.
The vibrant proteas
dance.
The Galjoens
swim.
The yellowwoods
stand strong.
While the African sun
greets us with a;
Sanibonani,
Dumelang,
Molo,
Hallo,
Hello,
Dumela,
Avuxen,
Ndaa,
Aa.
The choirs sing,
"Stimela siphum'eSouthAfrica"
From the highveld of
Limpopo to the mountains
of the Cape,
From the CBD
of Joburg
to the townships
of Khayelitsha,
Black,
White,
Indian,
Mixed.
We are all one,
one country
one nation
one family

All 64,007,187
of us,
we are One

Verhonger

Ek is van aanraking verhonger.
Van veilige drukkies
was ek geroof.
Nou kan ek nooit genoeg
hande vashou,
veilige soentjies
of harespeel
kry nie.
Ek is van aanraking verhonger-
en nou sal ek nooit
weer heel wees nie.

Die Duiwel

Ek het al die duiwel ontmoet
toe ek nog klein was.
Maar-
hy het nie
horiings,
n' drietand
of stert nie.
Nee-
hy was in my onderbewusheid,
in beheer van my denke.
Hy het vir my fluister
dat ek nie goed genoeg was nie.
Ek het al die duiwel ontmoet,
en sy naam was depressie

Acknowledgements

To my mom and dad:

Mommy, thank you for sharing your passion for literature with me and getting me my first thesaurus. Thank you for the editing and constructive criticism on all my work and for always being there for me. Thank you for sitting down at the dining room table and editing this anthology.
Pappa, thank you for always listening to me ramble, whether that be about my day or about whatever hyper fixation I have at the time. Thank you for always making me laugh, even if it's the last thing I feel like doing.
To you both, thank you for always protecting me and sheltering to the best of your abilities. Thank you for the amazing school, the laptop which I used to write this anthology with, the unconditional love and support for every project. I love you both more than any words or poems could ever express.

To Milan:

You have truly become my person. You're my "I'm only telling you this" friend and the girl I can yap to without any social battery. You always have a way of making me feel seen and loved through all the tough times. Love you lots <3

To Kirstin:

My sister from another family. You were the first friend I made after moving across the country. As much as I love to tease and irritate you about everything, you and your house will always be the safe place I run to whenever life gets too overwhelming <3

To Eben and Ryely:

You two are the best siblings an older sister could have ever asked for. Eben, as much as I would love to strangle you from time to time, you really are the best and I love you unconditionally and nothing will ever change that. Ryely, I know you're too little to understand everything in this anthology but I hope that one day when you're old enough you can look back and see what a huge impact you had on this book. I prayed to God for a little sister and, although I got 9 years late, I thank God every day that He gave me you <3

To Thea:

Bestie, you have, from the very beginning, read every piece of little writing I have given you and engaged fully in it. It is that, that gave me the confidence I needed to keep going. Thank you for all the English doubles where we always came out with sore sides from laughing all the way through <3

To Karen:

You were my first friend. You had every chance to choose popularity and all the boys over our friendship and yet you never once did. If it weren't for you, I wouldn't be here, never mind this anthology, so you are as much a part of this as I am <3

To Mrs. Le Roux:

You were my grade 8 English teacher and watched me go through all the ups and downs of that year. From depression and epileptic flareups to making new friends and growing into the person I am today. Your consistent belief in my writing and praise as well as helpful tips and tricks is what lead me to become the writer I am today. In grades 9 and 10 you were my history teacher and I couldn't have asked for anyone better. You took my least favorite subjects and made it suddenly one of my favorites. Thank you for all your kind words and smiles that never failed to brighten my day <3

To Ms. Swanepoel:

You took over from Mrs. Le Roux as my English teacher from grades 9 to 10. You always had a listening ear to whatever problems I had going on and never once called Thea and I out for our giggling. You read each and every poem in this anthology and pushed me to publish it. Thank you for letting me go over the word limits for creative writing (I promise I'm getting better) and for always giving me a good giggle. <3

To Eben and Ryely:

You two are the best siblings an older sister could have ever asked for. Eben, as much as I would love to strangle you from time to time, you really are the best and I love you unconditionally and nothing will ever change that. Ryely, I know you're too little to understand everything in this anthology but I hope that one day when you're old enough you can look back and see what a huge impact you had on this book. I prayed to God for a little sister and, although I got 9 years late, I thank God every day that He gave me you <3

To Thea:

Bestie, you have, from the very beginning, read every piece of little writing I have given you and engaged fully in it. It is that, that gave me the confidence I needed to keep going. Thank you for all the English doubles where we always came out with sore sides from laughing all the way through <3

To Karen:

You were my first friend. You had every chance to choose popularity and all the boys over our friendship and yet you never once did. If it weren't for you, I wouldn't be here, never mind this anthology, so you are as much a part of this as I am <3

To Mrs. Le Roux:

You were my grade 8 English teacher and watched me go through all the ups and downs of that year. From depression and epileptic flareups to making new friends and growing into the person I am today. Your consistent belief in my writing and praise as well as helpful tips and tricks is what lead me to become the writer I am today. In grades 9 and 10 you were my history teacher and I couldn't have asked for anyone better. You took my least favorite subjects and made it suddenly one of my favorites. Thank you for all your kind words and smiles that never failed to brighten my day <3

To Ms. Swanepoel:

You took over from Mrs. Le Roux as my English teacher from grades 9 to 10. You always had a listening ear to whatever problems I had going on and never once called Thea and I out for our giggling. You read each and every poem in this anthology and pushed me to publish it. Thank you for letting me go over the word limits for creative writing (I promise I'm getting better) and for always giving me a good giggle. <3

About the Author

 Hi! My name is Annemie van Wyk and I wrote this Anthology. I was born on the 3rd November 2008 in South Africa. I learned to read when I was 5/6 years old and learnt how to write shortly after that. Writing has always been a way of escaping the world. I was eight when I was first diagnosed with petit Mal Epilepsy. I didn't understand exactly what was happening so my family and I called my seizures absences. Three years later I was diagnosed with both ADHD and Aspergers Syndrome (now known as autism spectrum disorder). This meant that I often had a lot of very intense emotions but didn't know how to deal with them nor express them properly. I used my characters from the stories I wrote to illustrate what I was feeling and poems as my way of expressing those emotions. In the end of 2021, beginning 2022, I had a severe epileptic flareup and was diagnosed with Temporal-Lobe Epilepsy as well as non-epileptic seizures as a result of anxiety. I've struggled with mental health all my life due to my neurodivergence and the bullying at school as a kid. I have made it my mission to ensure I can help as many people with their mental health as possible in my lifetime, starting with this anthology.

www.ingramcontent.com/pod-product-compliance
Lightning Source LLC
Chambersburg PA
CBHW061443050726

47593CB00004B/1446